Pebble
Plus

Famous Firsts

THE FIRST CARS

by Roberta Baxter

Consulting Editor: Gail Saunders-Smith, PhD

Consultant: Jonson Miller, PhD
Associate Teaching Professor of History and Science, Technology, and Society
Drexel University

CAPSTONE PRESS
a capstone imprint

Pebble Plus is published by Capstone Press,
1710 Roe Crest Drive, North Mankato, Minnesota 56003
www.capstonepub.com

Library of Congress Cataloging-in-Publication Data
Baxter, Roberta, 1952– author.
The first cars / Roberta Baxter.
pages cm.—(Famous firsts)
Summary: "Large photographs and simple text describe eight early cars"—Provided by publisher.
Includes bibliographical references and index.
ISBN 978-1-4914-0574-1 (hb)—ISBN 978-1-4914-0642-7 (pb)—ISBN 978-1-4914-0608-3 (eb)
1. Automobiles—Juvenile literature. 2. Automobiles—History—Juvenile literature. I. Title.
TL147.B38 2015
629.222—dc23 2014001789

Editorial Credits
Erika L. Shores, editor; Terri Poburka, designer; Svetlana Zhurkin, media researcher; Laura Manthe, production specialist

Photo Credits
Alamy: Old Paper Studios, cover; Corbis: Bettmann, 13, 15, 19, Minnesota Historical Society, 9; Newscom: akg-images, 7, Everett Collection, 17, Image Broker/David Chapman, 21, PA/United Archives/WHA, 11; Shutterstock: egd, 5

Note to Parents and Teachers

The Famous Firsts set supports national social studies standards related to science, technology, and society. This book describes and illustrates early cars. The images support early readers in understanding the text. The repetition of words and phrases helps early readers learn new words. This book also introduces early readers to subject-specific vocabulary words, which are defined in the Glossary section. Early readers may need assistance to read some words and to use the Table of Contents, Glossary, Read More, Internet Sites, Critical Thinking Using the Common Core, and Index sections of the book.

Printed in the United States of America in North Mankato, Minnesota.
032014 008087CGF14

Table of Contents

Car History

Did you ride in a car today? Today's cars look much different from early ones. Let's find out about the first cars.

Parking

Some of the earliest cars looked like train engines. They ran on steam. They couldn't go very far or climb hills.

Nicolas-Joseph Cugnot builds the first steam car.

1769

U PARENT

Electric Cars

In the 1800s people began making vehicles powered by electricity. Thomas Parker made the first four-wheeled electric car in 1884.

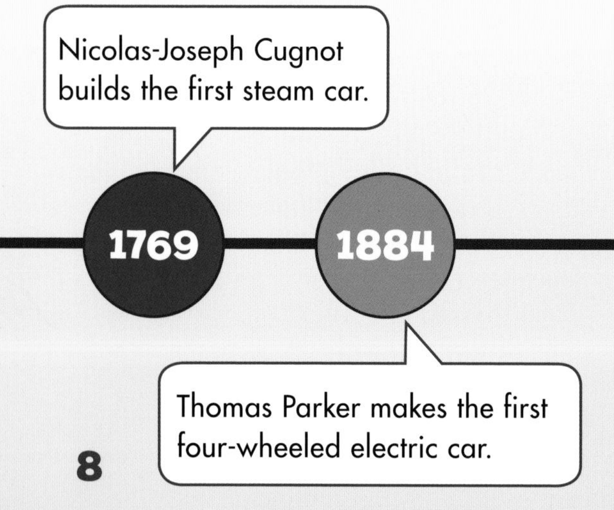
Nicolas-Joseph Cugnot builds the first steam car.
1769
1884
Thomas Parker makes the first four-wheeled electric car.

COLUMBIA PRINTING CO.
ENTERPRISE ENGRAVING CO.
VOLUNTEERS OF AMERICA
BERGER-KOHLSTEDT PRINTING CO.
COFFEE LUNCH ROOM
246
DOERR'S CIGARS

Gasoline Cars

Karl Benz put a gasoline engine on a three-wheeled carriage in 1885. Then in 1886 Gottlieb Daimler added one to a four-wheeled carriage.

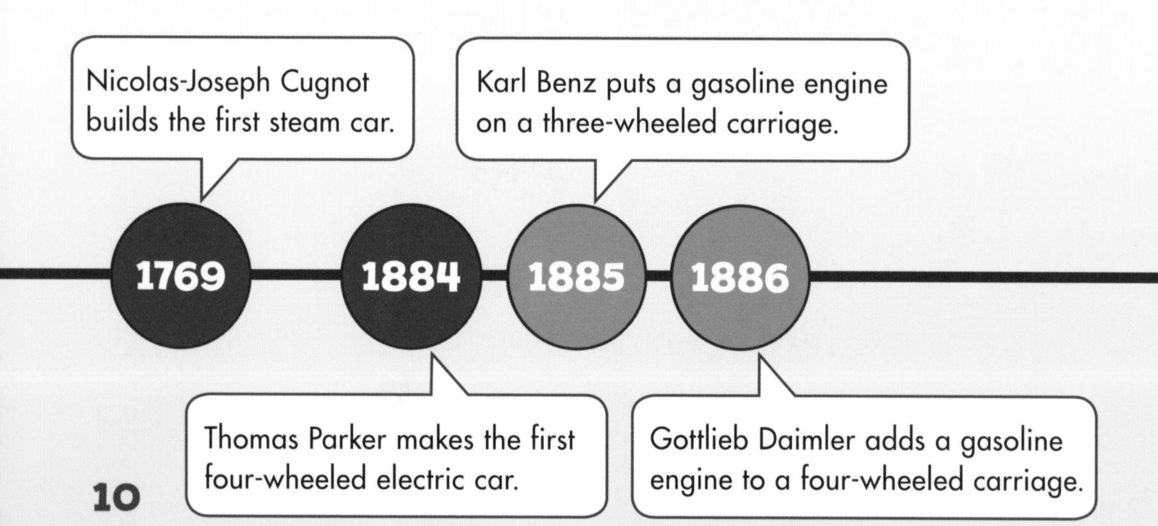
Nicolas-Joseph Cugnot builds the first steam car.
Karl Benz puts a gasoline engine on a three-wheeled carriage.
1769
1884
1885
1886
Thomas Parker makes the first four-wheeled electric car.
Gottlieb Daimler adds a gasoline engine to a four-wheeled carriage.

Karl Benz driving his three-wheeled carriage.

Car Racing

Six cars were in the first car race. Frank Duryea won in a car he built himself. It took almost 10 hours to drive 54 miles (87 kilometers) in a snowstorm.

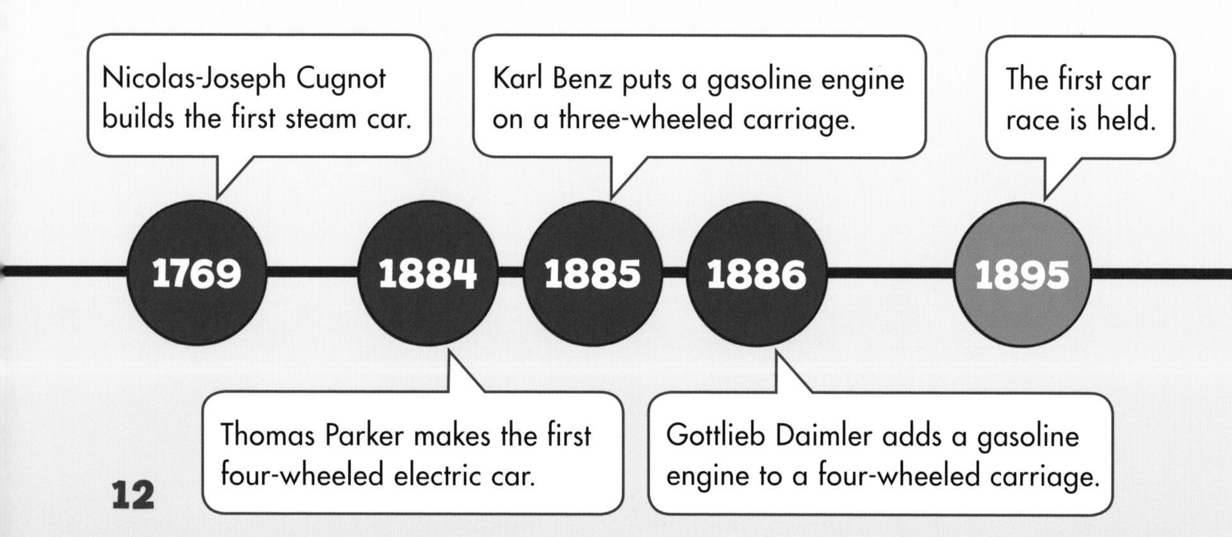
Nicolas-Joseph Cugnot builds the first steam car.
1769
Thomas Parker makes the first four-wheeled electric car.
1884
Karl Benz puts a gasoline engine on a three-wheeled carriage.
1885
Gottlieb Daimler adds a gasoline engine to a four-wheeled carriage.
1886
The first car race is held.
1895

5

Cars for Everyone

Early cars were expensive. They were made one at a time. Ransom Olds made thousands of cars in a factory. Olds was able to sell his cars for less money.

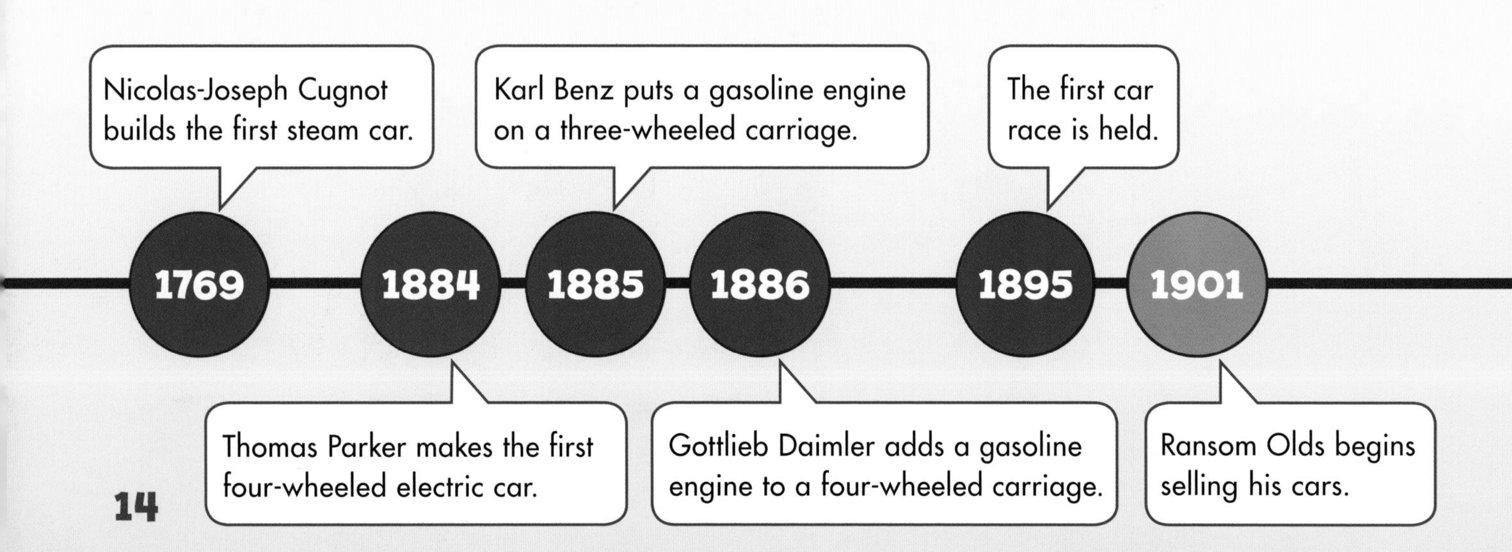
Nicolas-Joseph Cugnot builds the first steam car.
Karl Benz puts a gasoline engine on a three-wheeled carriage.
The first car race is held.
1769
1884
1885
1886
1895
1901
Thomas Parker makes the first four-wheeled electric car.
Gottlieb Daimler adds a gasoline engine to a four-wheeled carriage.
Ransom Olds begins selling his cars.

Roy Chapin drove an Oldsmobile from Detroit to New York City in 1902.

Henry Ford made the Model T in 1908. Ford's company first used the assembly line to make cars. Ford sold 15 million Model Ts.

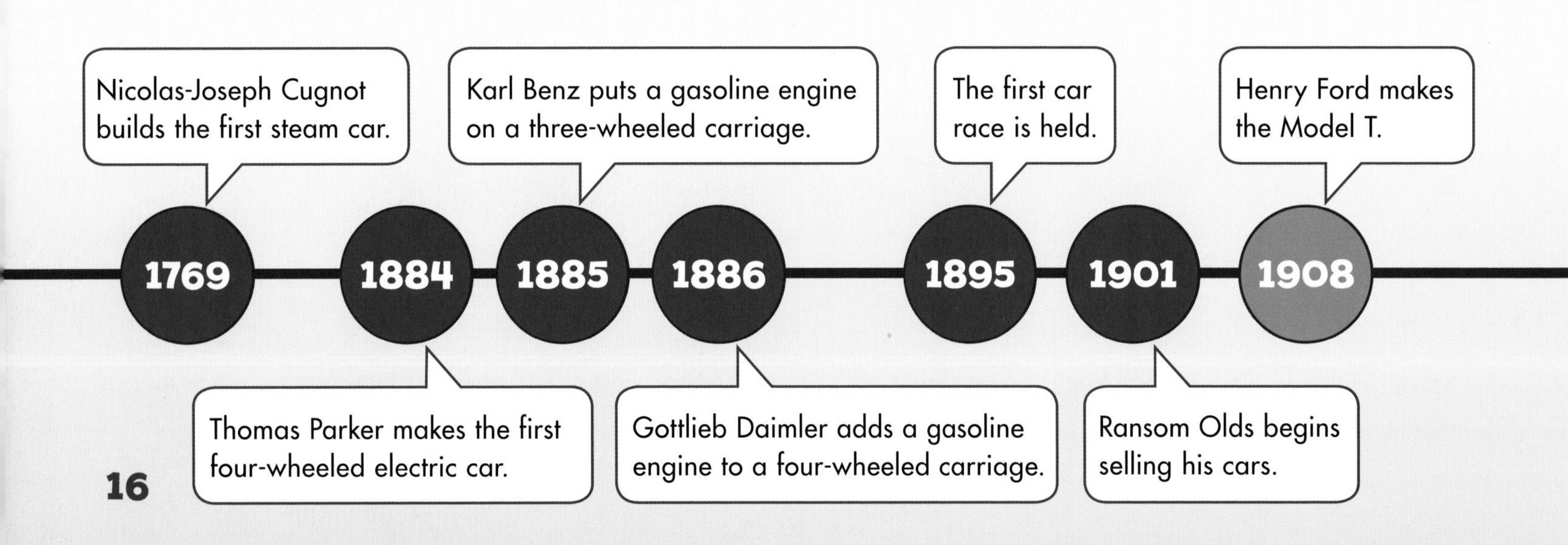
Nicolas-Joseph Cugnot builds the first steam car.
1769
Thomas Parker makes the first four-wheeled electric car.
1884
Karl Benz puts a gasoline engine on a three-wheeled carriage.
1885
Gottlieb Daimler adds a gasoline engine to a four-wheeled carriage.
1886
The first car race is held.
1895
Ransom Olds begins selling his cars.
1901
Henry Ford makes the Model T.
1908

The First Indy 500

A car called the Marmon Wasp won the first Indianapolis 500 race. Driver Ray Harroun drove at speeds of 75 miles (121 kilometers) per hour.

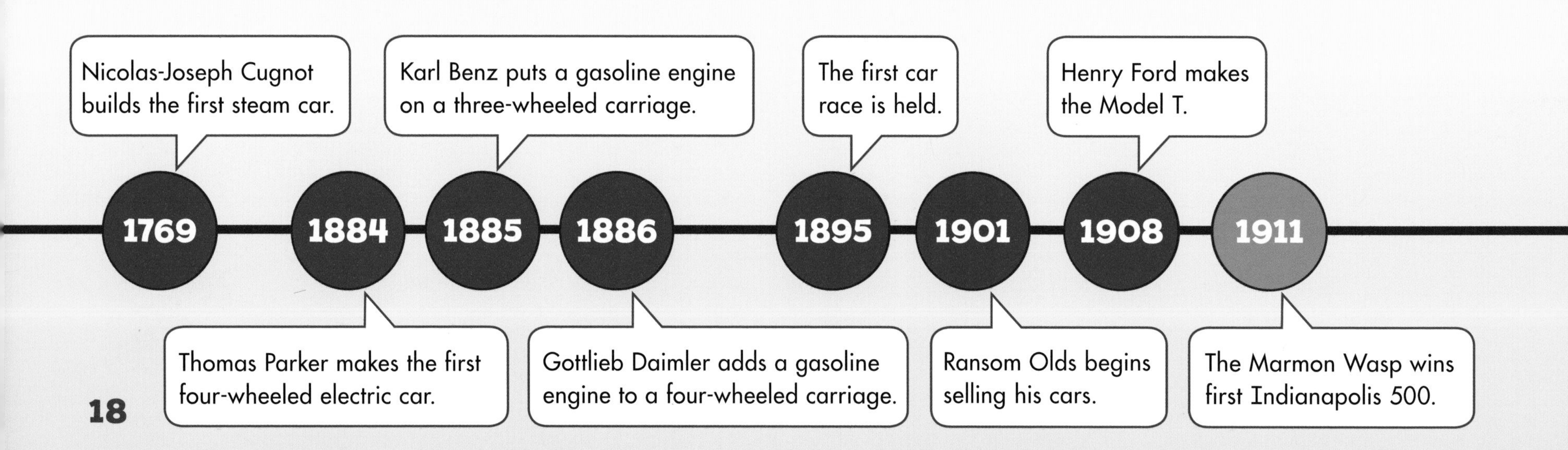
Nicolas-Joseph Cugnot builds the first steam car.
Karl Benz puts a gasoline engine on a three-wheeled carriage.
The first car race is held.
Henry Ford makes the Model T.
1769
1884
1885
1886
1895
1901
1908
1911
Thomas Parker makes the first four-wheeled electric car.
Gottlieb Daimler adds a gasoline engine to a four-wheeled carriage.
Ransom Olds begins selling his cars.
The Marmon Wasp wins first Indianapolis 500.

32
32

The First Muscle Car

Muscle cars are fast and powerful. In 1949 Oldsmobile began selling the Rocket 88. A big engine and lightweight body made it the earliest muscle car.

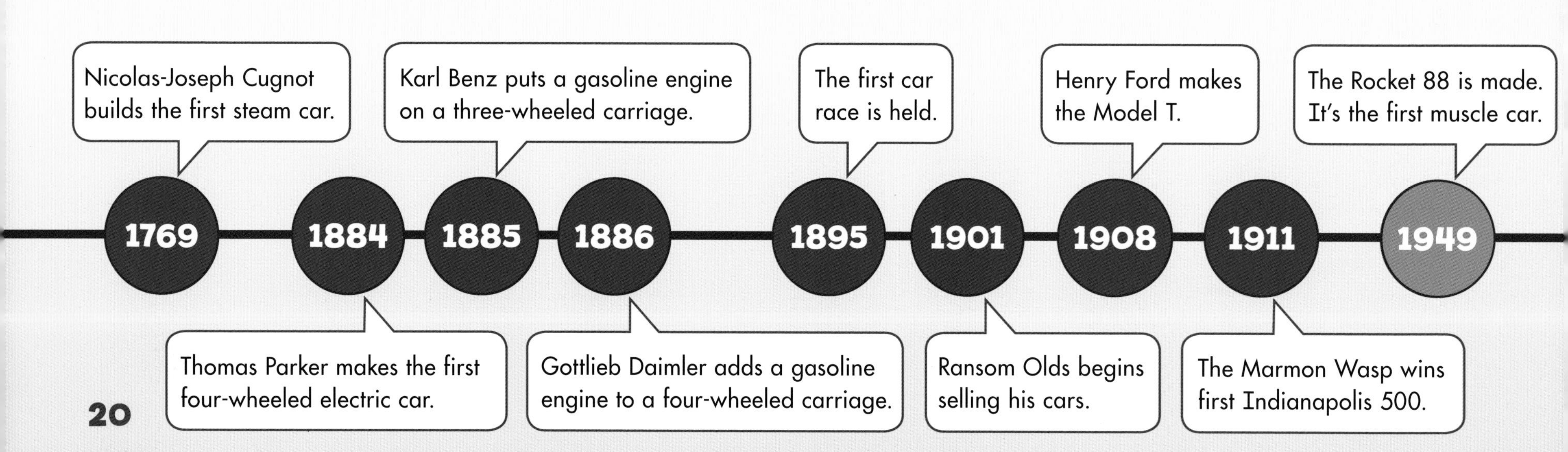

1769
Nicolas-Joseph Cugnot builds the first steam car.
1884
Thomas Parker makes the first four-wheeled electric car.
1885
Karl Benz puts a gasoline engine on a three-wheeled carriage.
1886
Gottlieb Daimler adds a gasoline engine to a four-wheeled carriage.
1895
The first car race is held.
1901
Ransom Olds begins selling his cars.
1908
Henry Ford makes the Model T.
1911
The Marmon Wasp wins first Indianapolis 500.
1949
The Rocket 88 is made. It's the first muscle car.

Glossary

assembly line—a way in which cars are made by many people putting on a single part as the car moves along to the next person

carriage—a cart with wheels usually pulled by horses

expensive—to cost a great deal of money

gasoline—fuel made from oil that can be used to make a car run

steam—water heated enough to turn into a gas

Read More

Abramovitz, Melissa. *Old Cars.* Cars, Cars, Cars. North Mankato, Minn.: Capstone Press, 2013.

Rau, Dana Meachen. *Cars.* We Go! New York: Marshall Cavendish Benchmark, 2010.

Roberts, Steven. *Henry Ford.* Jr. Graphic American Inventors. New York: PowerKids Press, 2013.

Internet Sites

FactHound offers a safe, fun way to find Internet sites related to this book. All of the sites on FactHound have been researched by our staff.

Here's all you do:

Visit *www.facthound.com*

Type in this code: 9781491405741

WWW.FACTHOUND.COM

Super-cool stuff!

Check out projects, games and lots more at
www.capstonekids.com

Critical Thinking Using the Common Core

1. Look at the photo on page 17. Use the photo to help you describe how an assembly line works. (Craft and Structure)

2. Look at the photos on pages 5 and 7. Describe some of the ways cars have changed over the years. (Integration of Knowledge and Ideas)

Index

Word Count: 222
Grade: 1
Early-Intervention Level: 20